# ALBANI GUID

*Your Ultimate Companion to Discovering Hidden Gems and Rich Heritage in 2024*

**Brooke Berry**

# Table of Contents

# CHAPTER ONE

## INTRODUCTION

Take off on an amazing tour across Europe's undiscovered jewel, where wild landscapes collide with a rich tapestry of culture and history. Greetings from Albania, a rising star in the travel industry that entices travelers with its enticing Ionian and Adriatic coasts, fascinating Ottoman and Communist legacies, and the breathtaking grandeur of the

Albanian Alps—the eerie Accursed Mountains.

Enter the pages of this travel guide and picture yourself hiking across the rough terrain of the Albanian Alps, a paradise for hikers looking for a nature unspoiled by time. Imagine valleys covered in a bright carpet of wildflowers, with lynxes moving gracefully through forests of spruce trees. Despite their intimidating name, the Accursed Mountains conceal an enchanted world for anyone seeking an adventure off the usual route.

Albania is a destination that is more popular than it used to be despite being neglected more often. Explore the echoes of its multifaceted past, where Communist tales and Ottoman influences collide. Explore settlements that date back hundreds of years, each telling a story of resiliency and custom. Albania presents its treasures to the world, now more accessible thanks to new air routes like Ryanair and Wizz Air.

Come along on a virtual journey through this treasure of the Balkans, where the excitement of adventure meets the warmth of welcome. Albania welcomes you if you're an experienced traveler or a wanderlust-stricken person, providing an immersive experience that goes beyond the typical. Use this guide as your compass to discover the mysteries of a country that is positioned to become the next popular travel destination. Welcome to the enchantment of Albania in 2024, where your adventure begins.

## Brief Overview of Albania

Nestled in the center of the Balkans, Albania presents itself as an undiscovered gem, just waiting to be unearthed by adventurous travelers looking for a genuine, off-the-beaten-path adventure. The beauty of the nation is found not only in its breathtaking natural surroundings, which include stunning beaches along the Adriatic and Ionian coasts but also in its intricate historical background, which is intertwined with elements of Communist and Ottoman influence.

## Exposing the Cursed Mountains: A Masterwork of Nature

The Accursed Mountains, a stunning range of jagged karst peaks that go by this ominous name, are a mesmerizing feature of Albania. But those who go to these heights are not cursed; rather, they are rewarded with breathtaking views of valley bottoms painted with a vibrant mosaic of wildflowers and lynxes strolling gracefully through ancient spruce woodlands. The Albanian Alps are a dream destination for avid hikers and nature lovers, providing challenging trails, breathtaking vistas, and the cozy welcome of traditional homestays.

## Uncovering Albania's Secrets: Reachable and Appealing

Albania is inviting visitors to immerse themselves in its rich tapestry as it sheds its shroud of secrecy and opens up more than ever. Today, convenient connections between Albania and locations like Edinburgh, Manchester, Stansted, Birmingham, and Liverpool are offered by major airlines such as Ryanair and Wizz Air. The capital city of Albania, Tirana, serves as the perfect starting point for a tour that takes in medieval castles, historic sites, and unspoiled natural gems.

## A Diverse Range of Encounters

This travel guide invites you to go with us as we unravel the secrets of Albania, a country that seamlessly blends the traditional and the modern. Explore winding streets lined with historically significant buildings, bask in the warmth of its vibrant culture, and journey through environments that range from sunny beaches to wild, untamed alpine landscapes. Discover why Albania is hailed as Europe's rising star in the pages that follow. It promises a journey filled with surprises, cultural diversity, and the pleasure of travel.

# What Makes Albania a Unique Destination

Nestled in the heart of the Balkan Peninsula, Albania offers a breathtaking mosaic of contrasts. Albania reveals itself as a varied gem, from the sun-kissed beaches along its Adriatic and Ionian coastlines to the rugged landscapes of the Accursed Mountains in the north. This is a nation where the heritage of the Ottoman Empire blends with contemporary appeal, and old history meets modern allure. Its uniqueness is enhanced by the varied scenery, extensive history, and kind friendliness.

## The Cursed Mountains: The Albanian Alps

The natural magnificence of the Albanian Alps, sometimes known as the Accursed Mountains, entices adventure seekers. Hikers and lovers of nature will find themselves in a dreamlike environment as jagged karst peaks pierce the sky. This place, essentially undiscovered by traditional tourists, is a haven for those looking for exceptional and unspoiled landscapes. Travel through valleys dotted with a riot of wildflowers and into spruce woodlands where lynxes roam free. A retreat into a pristine setting, the Accursed Mountains provide a stark contrast to the bustling cities.

## Cultural Mosaic: Communist and Ottoman Legacy

Albania's history unfolds like a gripping book, with layers of Communist and Ottoman influences sculpting the country's cultural landscape. The streets are lined with buildings from the Ottoman period, and there are still traces of the Soviet era. Discover Albania's rich history by exploring communist-era bunkers, Ottoman mosques, and ancient castles. This blending of cultures creates a special atmosphere where long-standing customs coexist with the spirit of a resilient nation.

## Ionian and Adriatic Coasts: Rivieras and Further Out

The Adriatic and Ionian Seas that hug Albania's coastline provide a beach experience that is comparable to that of its Mediterranean neighbors. The Riviera is a haven for sun worshippers, with its stunning beaches and azure waters. But beyond the well-known Riviera is a stretch of coastline home to charming villages, hidden coves, and ancient ruins. Discover the well-preserved Ottoman architecture of Gjirokastër, a town designated by UNESCO, or unwind in Dhermi, a coastal resort where crystal-clear waters meet olive trees.

## Emerging Travel Market

Albania's appeal is increased by the fact that its tourism industry is still in its infancy. Discovering uncharted territory and forming authentic connections with people are opportunities for visitors. Albania offers a more private experience where visitors can fully immerse themselves in the genuine warmth of the people and the unspoiled beauty of the countryside, in contrast to busy tourist destinations.

## Connectivity and Access

More flights from major European cities are now available to Albania, making it easier to reach than before. Tirana, the capital, welcomes visitors with a vibrant ambiance that blends modernity and tradition. Albania is a tempting location for travelers looking for a unique European experience away from the beaten path because of how easy it is to get there.

## Culinary Delights: A Culinary Adventure

For those looking for a true gourmet experience, Albanian cuisine is a wonderful find. The fusion of Balkan and Mediterranean influences creates a flavorful and vibrant culinary scene. Savor regional specialties like 'Byrek,' a savory pastry filled with cheese and herbs, or inhale the fragrances of grilled meats as they roast. Fresh seafood abounds in coastal locations, while substantial meals may fuel your activities in alpine settings.

## Friendliness and Warmth

Albania is renowned for its people's sincere compassion and friendliness. Locals are eager to share their stories and traditions and welcome visitors with open arms. Talk to people, and you will be invited to people's homes for homemade dinners or customary coffee. Travelers are left with enduring memories of camaraderie and warmth as a result of this genuine connection with the locals.

## A Secret Treasure Revealed

Albania pays homage to the beauty of uncharted territory; it is sometimes called Europe's secret gem. Its exceptional blend of natural wonders, rich cultural diversity, and the sincere friendliness of its people make for an unmatched vacation experience. Albania invites you to discover its secrets and be enchanted by its unique appeal, whether your goals are an adventure in the mountains, relaxation on stunning beaches, a gourmet journey through diverse cuisines, or an immersion in local hospitality. This book will be your guide as you peel back the layers of Albania, offering an authentic and engaging look at this hidden gem.

# CHAPTER TWO

## Albanian Alps: The Accursed Mountains

Set off on a daring expedition into the heart of Albania, where your research will be met by the magnificent Albanian Alps—ominously dubbed the Accursed Mountains. This rugged region with its jagged karst peaks, pristine spruce forests, and blooming valley bottoms is a haven for anybody looking for an adventurous getaway in the heart of Europe's rising star. Explore the allure of the Accursed Mountains, a precious natural gem tucked away in Albania's northern region. Discover the breathtaking landscape that has been shaped by time, where lynxes roam freely and wildflowers create a vibrant tapestry over the valleys.

## Hiking Trails and Adventures

Take out on a life-changing journey along the fabled Peaks of the Balkans Trail, which passes through the stunning regions of Kosovo, Montenegro, and Albania.

The trail, widely acclaimed as a hiker's dream come true, unveils a multifaceted mosaic of scenic natural features and cultural encounters.

## A Brief Overview of the Trail

Learn about the significance and background of the Balkans Trail's peaks. Recognize how it developed from a neighborhood trail to a globally renowned hiking path. Find more about the collaborative efforts of communities from different countries to preserve and promote this special route.

The story embedded in the very fabric of the Balkan Peninsula, the Peaks of the Balkans Trail is more than just a path that crosses the Albanian Alps. You enter a realm where culture and environment coexist as you set off on this amazing journey. This road links diverse landscapes and secret experiences, shaped by the combined vision of communities in Albania, Montenegro, and Kosovo.

## Highlights and Trail Sections

Discover the many sections of the trail, each offering a unique mix of activities and landscapes. Hikers may expect a wide range of attractions, from the stunning Valbona Pass to the vibrant Theth Valley. Extensive analyses of significant route segments establish the mood for an incredible adventure.

Towering peaks envelop you as you cross the Valbona Pass, providing a breathtaking backdrop for an extraordinary trek. Hikers are lured to explore the hidden corners of the Theth Valley, which unfolds like a storybook with its quaint hamlets and ancient traditions. Every section of the walk offers a fresh chapter, providing a spiritual journey in addition to a physical one.

## Ready: Crucial Hiking Advice

Get ready for your hike by following these helpful tips for selecting the right equipment. Regardless of experience level, this section provides essential information on gear requirements for an enjoyable and secure trip across the Albanian Alps.

## Selecting the Appropriate Equipment

Examine your options for hiking equipment, such as durable boots and small backpacks. Recognize the value of selecting equipment that suits your preferences and the particular challenges of the Balkans Trail's Peaks.

Selecting the right equipment for an epic journey is similar to selecting a companion. Robust, well-fitting boots become your reliable travel companions, carrying you across gurgling creeks and over difficult terrain. An appropriately stocked backpack that is heavy enough to allow for easy movement but yet contains all the essentials becomes an extension of your journey. Every piece of equipment chosen is essential to guaranteeing a faultless and enjoyable journey, from reliable water filtration to moisture-wicking clothing that adapts to changing weather conditions.

## Climatic and Seasonal Factors

Learn how the weather in the Albanian Alps varies and how this affects the best times to hike the region. Whether you like winter's snowy vistas or spring's blooms, careful planning ensures an enjoyable and well-organized trip.

Even though they are breathtaking in all seasons, the Albanian Alps reveal new aspects of their majesty every month. With wildflowers covering the plains and snow-capped peaks creating a dramatic contrast with the turquoise sky, spring promises a blast of color. Hikers may explore higher heights in the summer, when alpine vegetation is in full flower and breathtaking views stretch for miles. Autumn casts a golden light over the landscape, making the experience more peaceful and alone. For those looking for a challenging and unusual journey, the trail becomes an amazing paradise even in the winter with its frozen scenery.

## Trail Etiquette and Immersion in Culture

Become well-versed in the principles of responsible hiking, emphasizing the need of leaving no trace behind. Learn how hikers may contribute to the preservation of the trail's beautiful scenery and forge positive relationships with the people they encounter along the way.

## Valuing Local Communities and the Environment

Discover the rich cultural tapestry that is interwoven along the journey. Eat authentic cuisine, get to know the local cultures, and interact with traditional mountain people in a respectful manner. Hikers are given advice in this section on how to enhance their experience via cultural immersion.

A commitment to Leave No Trace principles serves as a compass to guide you as you go cautiously through the pristine landscapes. Respect for the nature and the people who live in these mountains go hand in hand. Experiences are deepened by the generation-to-generation transmission of local customs and traditions. Hikers may connect with the soul of the Albanian Alps via cultural immersion experiences, such as sharing a meal with a mountain family or taking part in a customary event.

**Trailside Cultural Encounters**

The Peaks of the Balkans Trail offers insights into the region's rich cultural fabric in addition to its scenic splendor. Discover regional customs, taste unusual cuisine, and get knowledge of traditional mountain settlements. Hikers may learn how to respectfully engage with the cultural heritage woven throughout the trail from this section.

The path is a cultural pilgrimage rather than just a physical one. Take part in animated conversations with residents in the center of Theth and discover stories carved into each stone of the historic structure. The air is filled with the inviting scents of traditional cuisine, luring you in to enjoy the comforts of a long-standing culture. Events, celebrations, and everyday life weave themselves into the vibrant tapestry of your hiking journey.

# Trekking Agencies and Guided Tours

This section offers crucial advice on selecting trustworthy trekking providers for those seeking guided tours. Hiking is a fun and perfect experience with insights into tour operators, whether you choose for a fully-supported walk or a self-guided adventure.

## Selecting an Appropriate Tour Operator

Make sure the tour operator you choose fits your expectations and interests by navigating the array of options available. This section offers useful advice on choosing the right experience, whether you want a group outing or something more personalized.

Selecting a tour operator is like hiring a guide for your travels; a knowledgeable travel companion who understands the intricacies of the itinerary. Your experience is defined in large part by factors including group size, itinerary flexibility, and guide expertise. Expert hikers' perspectives and their interactions with different operators provide important angles that assist you in making a choice that aligns with your ideal hiking experience.

## Individual Testimonials and Accounts

Take a virtual tour via hikers' first-hand stories and testimonials. For those who want to be hikers, these narratives provide insight into the many challenges and experiences encountered along the route, providing motivation and useful suggestions.

The Peaks of the Balkans Trail transforms from a route on a map to a tale of shared experiences as you read the accounts of others who have gone before you. The trail's essence is best expressed via firsthand accounts, which highlight the trail's friendship, breathtaking beauty, and triumphs against adversity. Each testimonies bears testament to the Albanian Alps' transformative power.

## Emergency Readiness and Safety

Arm yourself with knowledge on overcoming common obstacles on your journey, like as steep climbs and river crossings. This section offers feasible advice on how to overcome obstacles without sacrificing enjoyment or safety.

## Trail Challenges to Navigate

Learn how to deal with obstacles including river crossings, high elevations, and bad weather. Practical advice ensures that hikers are well equipped for the various terrains of the Balkan Trail's Peaks.

The road, although attractive, is not without its difficulties: a swift river that must be crossed carefully, a steep ascent that calls for strength, or an unforeseen shift in the weather that necessitates making snap decisions. Hikers may handle these issues safely using the information provided in this section. Every insight is a weapon in your toolbox, helping to ensure that the trials of the path become stepping stones to a deeper relationship with the natural world. Examples of these include assessing river currents and pacing yourself on ascents.

## Communication and Emergency Protocols

Put safety first by being well-versed in emergency procedures and communication strategies. Hikers may receive advice on avoiding dangers and obtaining assistance when needed, regardless of whether they are dealing with unforeseen weather changes or mild illnesses.

Although safety is paramount, being aware of emergency protocols enables hikers to respond appropriately to unforeseen circumstances. This chapter provides a comprehensive approach to maintaining your own and your fellow hikers' safety, covering everything from basic first aid practices to communication strategies in areas with spotty internet access. The

Peaks of the Balkans Trail is an experience that can be made safe and pleasurable with the right planning and knowledge.

## Your Balkan Peaks Adventure Is Here

As we get to the conclusion of our exploration of the Peaks of the Balkans Trail, imagine the incredible adventures that lay ahead for daring hikers. Every stop along this path is a celebration of nature and diversity of culture, from breathtaking vistas of the mountains to engaging with local traditions. This section should inspire you to go on a life-changing journey across the stunning Albanian Alps scenery, regardless of your level of experience. Put on your hiking boots, delve into the unknown, and let the Balkan Peaks lead you to an incredible journey.

## Wildlife Encounters in Spruce Forests

The virgin spruce forests of the Albanian Alps, which are sometimes shrouded in mystery, lure nature enthusiasts into a realm of remarkable variety. A symphony of nature greets us as we descend into the heart of these ancient woods, where lynxes roam soundlessly, brown bears stroll through thickets, and a multitude of bird species fill the sky.

## Spruce Forests' Ecological Significance

Learn about the ecological significance of the Albanian Alps' spruce woods. Recognize the delicate balance that keeps these ecosystems alive, supporting a variety of flora and animals and enhancing the overall environmental health of the area.

The towering trees and lush undergrowth of spruce forests are essential to maintaining the Albanian Alps' ecological equilibrium. These ecosystems serve as hotspots for biodiversity, offering a wide variety of species of food and habitat. Everything in these old forests, from large monsters to tiny insects, is a part of the complex web of life. Knowing the ecological significance of spruce forests provides the foundation for understanding how all living things are interrelated in these habitats.

- The Mysterious Phantom of the Forest: The Lynx

Take a virtual trip to discover the secrets of the Balkan lynx, a sly cat species that lives in the spruce forests. Find more about the behavioral patterns, ecological significance, and conservation initiatives aimed at protecting this fascinating predator.

With grace and mystery, the Balkan lynx glides through the dense spruce forests. It is a master of stealth and camouflage. Discover the secrets of this elusive feline as we examine its preferences for habitat, tactics for hunting, and challenges it faces in a constantly shifting landscape. The Balkan lynx conservation efforts provide insight into the precarious equilibrium that exists between human activities and the survival of this endangered species.

- Brown Bears: Stately Keepers of the Forest

Explore the world of brown bears, the majestic guardians of Albania's rural areas. Learn about their behaviors, their place in the ecology, and the conservation efforts aimed at preserving bears and humans coexisting.

Brown bears, with their massive stature and stomping gait, are essential to the spruce woodlands' biodiversity. Discover these omnivores' way of life, from foraging for fruit to engaging in amusing pranks. The importance of sustainable tourism and sustainable practices in protecting bear populations and their pristine environments is highlighted by conservation programs.

**Avian Wonders: Woodpeckers, Songbirds, and Raptors**

- Aerial Ballets in the Skies: Raptors Soaring High

Gaze above and see the flying raptor ballets that adorn the Albanian Alps. Discover the many varieties of raptors that soar via the thermals above the spruce forests, contributing to the area's rich birdlife.

From the powerful golden eagle to the agile peregrine falcon, the spruce forests provide an excellent habitat for a variety of raptors. Explore the world of these avian predators, learning about their hunting techniques, nest-building schedules, and vital roles in maintaining the ecological balance. The wide variety of raptors that live in the Albanian Alps will inspire both environmentalists and enthusiasts of bird watching.

- Forest Drummers: Woodpeckers

Descend from the clouds to the intricate world under the canopy, where the forest's drummers, the woodpeckers, play their rhythms. Learn about the several kinds of woodpeckers that inhabit spruce forests and their unique adaptations.

The woodpecker's bright plumage and distinctive drumming noises provide a symphony of sounds to the peaceful spruce woodlands. Learn about their methods of foraging, how they build their nests, and how important it is for the forest ecosystem to remain healthy. Every species contributes to the vibrant and expanding forests, whether it is via the acrobatic displays of the lesser spotted woodpecker or the rhythmic tapping of the black woodpecker.

- Songbirds: Songs Between the Leaves

As the air fills with the entrancing harmonies of songbirds, pay close attention to the musical tones resonating amid the spruce trees. Discover the wide variety of songbird species that inhabit the

Albanian wilderness and provide melodies to the forest atmosphere.

The songbirds of the Albanian Alps provide a serene backdrop to the clean spruce forests, with their melodious calls ranging from the beautiful nightingale voice to the exuberant tweeting of the finches. Recognizing and appreciating the diverse songs and vivid plumage of the many songbird species will satisfy nature enthusiasts and birdwatchers. Realizing the significance of these avian inhabitants heightens our consciousness of the precarious equilibrium present in the forest ecosystem.

## Insect Life and Forest Floor Microcosms

- A Rainbow of Colors: Butterflies and Beetles

Go down to the forest floor and take in the beetles and butterflies' rainbow of colors. Discover the abundance of insects that thrive in the little worlds under the massive spruce trees and add to the intricate web of life.

Many butterflies and beetles find the lush foliage and abundant flora of the spruce forests to be ideal habitats. Explore the world of these decomposers and pollinators, learning about their ecological roles and the symbiotic relationships that develop in the forest's underbrush. The vibrant colors of butterflies and the hardworking beetles provide excitement and vitality to the rich forest floor tapestry.

- Microbiology and Fungi: Custodians of Biodiversity

Discover the fascinating world of bacteria and fungi that are essential to maintaining the richness and general health of spruce forests. Discover the intricate equilibrium within the microcosms under our feet, the symbiotic relationships between fungi and trees, and the decomposition process.

A world of fungi and bacteria lives underneath the tall spruce trees, silently enhancing the forest's whole life cycle. Explore the intricacies of mycorrhizal networks, which are networks of fungi that symbiotically interact with tree roots to enhance nutrient absorption and maintain the general health of the forest. Observe the fascinating world of decomposition, where organic components and falling leaves combine to form the foundation of new life. The intricate dance of life inside the microcosms of the forest floor is revealed by comprehending the roles played by fungi and microorganisms.

## Problems and Initiatives in Conservation

- Conservation Challenges: Preserving Biodiversity

Face the conservation issues that threaten the fragile species balance in the spruce forests. Examine the effects of climate change, deforestation, and human activity on the Albanian Alps' animals and vegetation. The pristine state of the spruce forests faces several issues, such as habitat loss and the effects of climate change. Recognize how interconnected these issues are and the cumulative effects they have on the region's biodiversity. To guarantee the ongoing health of the spruce forests and the many species that depend on them, conservation efforts become crucial in reducing these problems.

- Collaborative Approach to Community-Led Conservation

Learn about the possibilities of locally driven conservation initiatives that strengthen local to train the locals to be land stewards. Examine case studies and success stories where local populations actively participate in preserving the Albanian Alps' biodiversity.

Local populations emerge as crucial allies in preserving the spruce forests' biodiversity in the face of conservation issues. Locals become advocates for reforestation projects, sustainable practices, and the preservation of important ecosystems via concerted efforts. Case studies from the Albanian Alps demonstrate the benefits of community-led conservation and indicate that human activity and the preservation of a pristine environment may coexist together.

## Guidelines for Visitors and Conscientious Travel

- Conserving Environment: Principles for Conscientious Travel

Set out on an exploration of responsible tourism as we look at suggestions for visitors who want to take in the splendor of the spruce forests without endangering their delicate ecosystems. These guidelines provide visitors with the tools they need to become responsible environmental stewards, from ethical wildlife viewing to the Leave No Trace philosophy.

Ensuring that future generations may appreciate the spruce forests' natural grandeur is contingent upon responsible tourism. Learn about ethical ways to observe animals, responsible hiking, and sustainable practices that lessen their impact on the environment. By following these guidelines, visitors foster an environmentally conscious culture and contribute to the preservation of the Albanian Alps.

- Unveiled: A Tapestry of Life

Imagine the complex tapestry of life that grows within this amazing environment as we continue to examine animal interactions in the spruce woodlands of the Albanian Alps. Every species in these old woods, from soaring eagles to beautiful butterflies and cunning lynxes, is vital to maintaining the delicate balance. The need for coordinated efforts to preserve this biodiversity is highlighted by the conservation challenges, guaranteeing that the spruce forests will continue to serve as a haven for animals and tourists who are eager to take in the wonders of nature. Whether you are an experienced naturalist or a curious tourist, this subchapter should help you better comprehend how all living things are related in the Albanian wilderness.

## Theth Village: Gateway to Peaks of the Balkans

Theth Village, Albania's hidden gem, is the ideal starting point for seeing the magnificent Peaks of the Balkans. It offers visitors looking for a unique blend of adventure, natural beauty, and cultural richness an experience that cannot be found anywhere. Theth is a fabled place hidden deep inside the Accursed Mountains, enthralling visitors with its immaculate landscape, historic structures, and kind welcome.

## Theth Village Introduction:

Theth Village is the starting place for hikers embarking on the Peaks of the Balkans trek, a well-known trail that winds through the breathtaking Albanian Alps. The village itself offers a distinctive glimpse into Albanian mountain life and is a timeless retreat, maintaining traditions dating back generations. A prominent medieval tower, verdant flora, and stone-roofed homes greet visitors approaching Theth, evoking a sense of tranquility and authenticity.

## Splendor in Nature:

Magnificent natural beauty, exemplified by rugged peaks, glistening streams, and verdant forests, envelops Theth. The Grunas Waterfall, a magnificent waterfall that adds to the allure of the surroundings, envelops the village. Hikers and lovers of the outdoors may discover the rich biodiversity found in the pristine landscapes, which are enhanced by unusual species and vegetation. The town, which is part of Theth National Park, is a haven for anybody looking for a harmonious blend of natural and cultural heritage.

**Traditional Wealth:**

Theth's commitment to preserving traditional Albanian culture is one of its unique features. Many historically significant Albanian tower homes, or Kullas, that have been conserved and showcase the region's architectural heritage may be found inside the hamlet. Staying in guesthouses run by friendly individuals allows visitors to fully immerse themselves in the local way of life. This promotes the local community's sustainability while also providing a real experience.

## The Balkan Trek's High Points:

For hikers embarking on the challenging but very rewarding Peaks of the Balkans trek, which crosses Albania, Kosovo, and Montenegro, Theth is an essential destination. Hikers will encounter a wide range of landscapes throughout the way, from rocky peaks to alpine meadows, providing them with a constantly shifting view. Depending on the path chosen, Theth marks the start or the conclusion of this amazing journey and provides a base for hikers to recuperate, refuel, and take in the hamlet's rich cultural diversity.

## Resident Hospitality and Gastronomy:

Not only is Theth Village known for its natural beauty, but its residents also provide a warm greeting. They welcome visitors with open arms and usually invite them to participate in storytelling sessions, traditional dances, and local festivals. The guesthouses in the area provide a taste of authentic Albanian cuisine, with hearty mountain dishes that showcase the creativity of the locals. For every visitor, the delight of enjoying a classic supper in such a beautiful setting becomes a priceless memory.

Theth Village continues to stand as a testament to Albania's allure, providing a captivating experience for those who are ready to take in the untamed splendor of the Accursed Mountains. Discoverers, wildlife enthusiasts, and connoisseurs of culture all fall in love with Theth, whether it is used as the jumping-off point or the end destination for the Peaks of the Balkans expedition. Visitors may interact with nature, history, and the welcoming character of the Albanian people at this place where time seems to stand still. Walking to Theth is more than just a physical journey—it's a voyage into the heart of Albania's wild surroundings.

# CHAPTER THREE

## Coastal Charms: Adriatic and Ionian Coasts

Discover the breathtaking beauty of Albania's Coastal Charms, where the Adriatic and Ionian Coasts blend to provide an enthralling landscape mosaic. Travelers seeking unspoiled natural riches and a hint of Mediterranean appeal flock to this charming spot nestled in the heart of the Balkans.

The Adriatic Coast invites visitors to unwind along its immaculate beachfront with its turquoise waters and stunning beaches. Every stretch of coastline, from the bustling beach towns to the remote coves, has a unique story to tell. Take a plunge into the glistening blue waters, enjoy the crisp sea breeze, and soak up the Mediterranean sun. Beyond the beaches, the coastal region is appealing due to its historic settlements and vibrant local culture, which provide depth to the experience.

There's something fresh to discover on the Ionian Coast. Picture yourself gazing upon breathtaking cliffs that give way to the sea, quaint fishing villages, and endless stretches of olive trees. The Ionian region enthralls with its own charm and carefree attitude. Take a stroll along charming lanes, savor regional cuisine at seaside tavernas, and watch the sunset over serene waters.

Albania's Coastal Charms provide a wide range of experiences, from serene retreats to colorful beach landscapes. The Adriatic and

Ionian shores provide an incredible journey along the shores of this rising star in European tourism, whether you're looking for adventure, relaxation, or a little of everything.

## Scenic Beauty and Beaches

Explore the azure magnificence of Albania's coastline, where a patchwork of stunning beaches is cradled by the Adriatic and Ionian Seas. Every stretch of beach has its own story to tell, from the reflected allure of Mirror Beach to the hidden treasures of Gjipe. This chapter will begin with a tour of the sun-drenched beachfront, where we will examine the benefits and drawbacks, distinguishing features, and expert advice for an amazing beach experience.

- Mirror Beach: A Treasure of the Mediterranean

Overview: Mirror Beach, a beloved local destination, beckons with reasonable prices, a delightful Mediterranean atmosphere, and pristine waters. It's safe, family-friendly, and has a beautiful background, which makes it great for swimming and photography.

**Advantages:**

- Family-friendly

-Beautiful environment

- Oceanfront restaurant and bar

- Crystal clear water

**Cons:**

- Sunbed and umbrella rentals are pricey.

**The Reasons We Suggest:**

Mirror Beach offers a perfect getaway with its sun-kissed waves, rock climbing opportunities, and seaside restaurants.

**Expert Tip:**

There's no need to cook—enjoy regional cuisine at the beachside bar and grill.

- Ksamil Beach: An Ionian Gem

Overview: Ksamil Beach is a European gem with white sand, azure waves, and breathtaking views. Even at busy times, it offers water sports and breathtaking sunsets.

**Advantages:**

Activities that are available in the water are

-Wonderful sunset vista

- Offshore islands

- Immaculate water

**Drawbacks:**

- Congested

**The Reasons We Suggest:**

Ksamil's calm waters and surrounding islands make it a family-friendly paradise, perfect for swimming.

**Expert Tip:**

For even more isolation, check out nearby abandoned islands.

- Charm in Pebbles: Dhīrmi Beach

Overview: Dhërmi Beach offers views of the sea and mountains, with its pebbly shoreline and gorgeous blue oceans. Even though it's crowded, it's great for snorkeling, swimming, and relaxing on a beach day.

**Advantages:**

-Views of the sea and mountains

- Immaculate waters

-Beach loungers are offered; they're perfect for a variety of water sports

**Cons:**

- Overcharging visitors for drinks

**The Reasons We Suggest:**

Dhërmi is a must-see because of its immaculate waters, beach amenities, and water sports.

**Expert Tip:**

To avoid crowds, go during the weekdays or off-seasons; June and September are great months to visit.

- Borsh Beach: Calm Haven

Overview: Albania's longest beach, Borsh Beach, offers a tranquil environment, excellent restaurants, and a turquoise sea. A serene retreat with plenty of space for relaxation.

## Advantages:

- Length and azure lake

- Excellent eateries and cafes

- Calm atmosphere

## The Reasons We Suggest:

Borsh is the perfect place to unwind because of its serene surroundings and historic landmarks.

## Expert Tip:

Take a trip back in time to the Middle Ages by visiting the neighboring Borsh Castle.

- Miniature Adventure at Gjipe Beach

Overview: Daring beachgoers will enjoy Gjipe Beach, which is tiny yet stunning. Only accessible by hiking or canoeing, it ensures an exceptional and unadulterated experience.

**Advantages:**

- Risk-taking entry

- Hydrating water

- Adjacent trails for hiking

**The Reasons We Suggest:**

Gjipe offers a secret haven for adventure-seeking nature lovers.

Expert Advice:

For a genuine experience, a tent in the area behind the beach.

- A Family Haven at Golem Beach

**Overview:** The second-largest coastline in Albania, Golem Beach is renowned for its white sand beach, abundant vegetation, and crescent shape. It offers a fun and secure experience and is easily accessible for families.

**Advantages:**

- A sandy shoreline

- Calm, shallow water - Facilities suitable for families

- Conveniently located

**The Reasons We Suggest:**

Golem is a family-friendly destination because of its well-kept amenities and gentle waves.

**Expert Tip:**

Look into nearby eateries to get a variety of food options.

- Vlore's Orikum Beach: Approachable Beauty

Overview: With its gravel beach and glistening clean sea, Orikum Beach is easily accessible and equipped with amenities for comfortable travel.

**Advantages:**

- Immaculate Water

- A grave coastline

- Launching a place for yachts

**The Reasons We Suggest:**

For a peaceful day, Orikum offers a lovely coastline with convenient amenities.

**Expert Tip:**

For a comfortable experience on the gravel seabed, use aqua shoes.

- Picture-Perfect Paradise: Jali Beach — Himarë

Overview: The picture-perfect resort of Jali Beach, sometimes called Jalë Beach, has crystal-clear, blue water. It attracts visitors from all over the world and is perfect for picture shoots and a variety of water activities.

**Advantages:**

- Stunning landscape - Perfect for pictures

- A range of aquatic activities

**The Reasons We Suggest:**

Jali Beach offers a wonderful seaside experience thanks to its stunning surroundings and plenty of activities.

**Expert Tip:**

Make use of the campsite for a full beach vacation that includes other sporting events.

- Himarë's Palasa Beach: Peace by the Sea

Overview: The stunning blue ocean at Palasa Beach, sometimes called Palase Beach, is complemented by a white sand

and gravel shoreline. The water is perfect for swimming and snorkeling since it is extremely clean.

**Advantages:**

- Wide beach

- Immaculate water - Ideal for tanning

**The Reasons We Suggest:**

Palasa is a nice refuge because of its serene surroundings and pristine seas.

**Expert Tip:**

Take a trip to the nearby Llogara National Park in addition to Palasa Beach.

- Laid-Back Seclusion at Buneci Beach, Himarë

Overview: Offering a more relaxed atmosphere, Buneci Beach, also known as Bunec Beach, is great for those looking for peace away from large crowds. It creates a peaceful environment with a blend of gravel and small stones.

**Advantages:**

A relaxed vibe, a cozy environment, and a peaceful location

**The Reasons We Suggest:**

The little setting of Buneci Beach offers a serene escape from stress.

**Expert Tip:**

The national road leads directly to Buneci Beach, which is situated between Piqeras and Lukove.

Set off on a seaside adventure as we uncover the unique characteristics and varied splendor of Albania's breathtaking beaches. Every beach has a story of natural wonders just waiting to be discovered, from family-friendly havens like Golem to hidden gems like Gjipe. Come along on this trip with us and take in Albania's stunning coastline scenery.

## Exploring Coastal Towns

Take a fascinating tour of Albania's sun-kissed coastline, where the Adriatic and Ionian shores support a string of coastal towns, each with a unique story to tell. The fascinating stories of Sarandë, Vlorë, Himarë, Dhermi, Ksamil, Orikum, Dhërmi Beach, Jali Beach, Palasa Beach, and Buneci Beach will be revealed to you as you delve deeper into this comprehensive exploration, revealing the layers of history, natural wonders, and modern allure that define these coastal treasures.

- Sarandë: A Balancing Act of Tradition and Modernity

The southern jewel of the Albanian Riviera, Sarandë, draws you into a perfect blend of historic ruins and vibrant coastal life. Explore the Butrint UNESCO World Heritage Site, where artifacts from long-gone civilizations whisper tales of grandeur. Ksamil's lively restaurants and seafood havens along the waterfront promenade, which serves as the backdrop for sunsets over the islands.

- Vlorë: A Seaside Crossroads in History

Vlorë is a monument of Albania's struggle for independence, its struggle being chronicled by the Museum of Independence and the Independence Monument. Discover Dhërmi's beaches, where leisure and history blend to create a serene environment ideal for introspection.

- Himarë: Calm Amidst Waves and Mountains

Cradled between the Ionian Sea and mountains, Himarë offers a peaceful haven. The peaceful rhythm of the waves creates a melody on remote beaches like Jali and Buneci, accessible via the cobblestone promenades of Old Town. With its stunning view of the town, the Ali Pasha Castle entices you to go through time.

- Dhermi: The Azure and Green Canvas of Nature

Where the sea meets lush landscapes, Dhermi spreads like a picture. Its coastline is a treasure, with gorgeous hills and glistening oceans. Adventure awaits in the Gjipe Canyon, a playground for nature enthusiasts seeking a closer relationship with the environment, beyond the picturesque Dhërmi Beach.

- Ksamil: Peaceful Islands

Ksamil is a picture-perfect location with friendly islands dotted across the horizon. The islands' remote beaches and hidden coves beckon you to swim at Mirror Beach's crystal-clear waters and unwind in the Mediterranean sun. In the seaside haven of Ksamil, time seems to stand still.

- Orikum: Discovering Coastal Adventures

The starting point for water activities on the Ionian coast is

Orikum. The spotless waters and gravel coastline of the beach entice those who like water sports to explore the wonders of the ocean. Set out on a leisurely cruise on your yacht or take a boat tour to nearby caves. The allure of Orikum lies not just in its stunning coastline but also in the array of activities available to ensure a fun beach getaway.

- Unraveling a Sun-Kissed Tapestry at Dhërmi Beach

Dhërmi Beach stretches out like a sun-kissed tapestry of golden sand. This almost kilometer-long beach provides enough space for those looking for peace and quiet. Swimmers are drawn to the sea's gentle waves, and beachfront amenities provide a leisurely day by the water.

- Jali Beach: A Redefining of Tranquility

Called Jalë Beach, Jali Beach invites holidaymakers looking for peace and quiet. Jali is tucked away from busy crowds and offers a more exclusive beach experience. The combination of white sand and gravel, together with the azure waters, provide a serene environment ideal for strolls and tanning.

- The Blue Symphony of Nature at Palasa Beach

Palasa Beach epitomizes the tranquility of nature with its turquoise oceans and white sand and pebble shoreline. Sun worshippers are encouraged to take a break on the wide shore, whether it's by spreading out a blanket or relaxing on a beach chair.

- Buneci Beach: An Unveiled Coastal Sanctuary

Buneci Beach, also referred to as Bunec Beach, offers a tranquil retreat for those looking for a more sedate beach getaway. Buneci exudes a carefree atmosphere away from busy people, where visitors may enjoy swimming, tanning, and spending time alone.

Take a comprehensive journey of Albania's coastal tapestry, where each town appears as a distinct chapter that invites you to savor the historical tales, the serenity of the environment, and the allure of the Albanian beach.

# Water Activities and Relaxation

Prepare yourself to immerse yourself in a chapter dedicated to the soothing rhythm of waves and the many water activities that await as you embark on your coastal vacation throughout Albania's Adriatic and Ionian Coasts. Albania offers a wide range of coastal activities, from thrilling adventures to peaceful relaxation, all along its sandy coastline.

## Beachside Excitations: An Adventure for Fans of the Water

In addition to being a stunning backdrop, the Albanian shoreline is a vibrant playground for thrill-seekers. Take a plunge into the glistening waters to enjoy a range of thrilling water sports. Paddle boating enables you to explore the coastline at your own pace, while jet-skiing offers an exhilarating experience as you slice through the waves. Try sea riding for a more relaxed experience that will allow you to work out while taking in the beauty of the coastline.

Snorkeling reveals a vibrant underwater world to those who have a penchant for exploring under the surface. Every snorkeling trip is an amazing experience due to the stunning display of marine life that abounds along the Albanian coast. The coastal waters of Albania provide something for every kind of water enthusiast, whether they an adrenaline enthusiasts or someone who appreciates the serene beauty of underwater ecosystems.

## Calm Havens: Sun-Kissed Shores and Unwinding

Among the exhilaration of aquatic activities, find your place on Albania's sunny beaches. Mirror Beach invites you to relax on its sandy beaches and is named for the beautiful way the sun reflects off its calm waves. Wander along Ksamil Beach and experience the warm embrace of white sand under your feet. The beach's turquoise waters and picturesque sunset vistas provide an enchanted haven.

Only reachable by hiking or canoeing, Gjipe Beach offers a tranquil getaway. This unspoiled gem serves as a haven for anyone looking for peace away from the bustling crowds. Jali Beach provides a serene environment for times of leisure with its glistening clean waters and expansive views. Renowned for its carefree vibe, Buneci Beach beckons with the prospect of a serene haven inside the embrace of nature.

## Best-Kept Secrets in Nature: Undiscovered Coves and Islands

Discover the lesser-known parts of Albania's coastline, where isolated islands and coves reveal the mysteries of nature. Nestled amid towering cliffs, Gjipe Beach offers rugged but beautiful landscapes that are only accessible by the most daring adventurer. Golem Beach is a small but charming beach with a crescent shape that is ideal for a family-friendly day at the beach. It is easily accessible.

Jali Beach, often referred to as Jalë Beach, is a stunning location for spending a day at the beach with loved ones. It's a varied place with pristine waterways and opportunities for kayaking, snorkeling, and exploring hidden tunnels. Buneci Beach's immaculate beauty provides a backdrop for times of meditation and relaxation for those seeking a more sedate holiday.

## Gourmet Pleasures: Dining By the Ocean

Enjoying the culinary specialties that define Albania's coastline makes no beach trip complete. Mirror Beach offers a delicious selection of regional food and fresh fish at its oceanfront restaurant and bar. Golem Beach offers the opportunity to sample a variety of cuisines while taking in the seaside scenery. It is encircled by vibrant cafés.

Eat the regional specialties that showcase the rich culinary tapestry of the area as you visit the beach towns. Every taste is an exploration of the gastronomic heritage of Albania's coastal villages, ranging from succulent fresh seafood to sweets with Mediterranean influences. Your beach getaway is enhanced by the unique eating experience created by the fusion of cuisine and water.

## Enchanting Dusks: Seizing Moments by the Water

Enjoy the romance of Albania's shoreline sunsets as the day gracefully ends and the nighttime arrives. Palasa Beach is the perfect setting for a lovely evening by the sea with its combination of white sand and rocks. Enjoy the rhythmic background of the gentle waves as you take in the splendor of the setting sun. With its breathtaking backdrop, Jali Beach transforms into a vibrant picture, providing the perfect setting for priceless memories.

Buneci Beach, known for its serene environment, invites you to see the breathtaking embrace of the sunset. A serene atmosphere is created by the way the light dances over the water and the soothing sounds of the sea. You'll be enveloped in a romantic hideaway as the sun sets, capturing moments that last long after the last rays of sunlight have faded.

## Coastal Wellbeing: Relaxing on the Beach

Beyond the allure of sun-kissed beaches and the thrill of water sports, Albania's coastline offers a special opportunity for coastal health. As you practice yoga on the beach, let the sound of the waves serve as your background music. Golem Beach's wide shoreline makes for a lovely setting for beachside yoga, allowing you to re-establish a connection with the natural world and revitalize your senses.

Think about all-inclusive trips offered by beachside resorts, where wellness programs and spa services are chosen to complement your beachside experience. Coastal wellness in Albania is a holistic experience that balances the mind, body, and spirit, offering anything from beach massages to guided meditation sessions. Take advantage of the sea's healing properties by setting off on a wellness-focused coastal vacation.

## Sea Adventures: Island Finder and Cruises

Island cruises and naval excursions can elevate your holiday by the water. Orikum Beach's gravel beach and glistening clean waters make it an excellent site to begin your marine adventure. Launch your vessel from this exquisite

See hidden caverns and secluded harbors while sailing the Ionian Sea from a beachside point.

Think of taking a trip to any of the nearby islands that border Albania's coastline. To make the most of your island-hopping holiday, Jali Beach offers camping in addition to its stunning coastline. Every island offers a fresh opportunity for exploration, from kayaking to snorkeling, bringing an extra level of thrill to your coastal trip.

## Unwinding and Exploration: Achieving Harmony by the Water

Albania's stunning coastline skillfully balances adventure and relaxation, providing each visitor with a wonderful experience. The Adriatic and Ionian Coasts invite you to discover a coastal paradise that pleases a wide range of interests, whether your preference is for the romanticism of sunset vistas, the serenity of peaceful beaches, or the adrenaline of water sports.

Allow the sea to guide you through a rich tapestry of experiences as you peruse this chapter on water sports and recreation. Albania's seaside attractions invite you to experience the spirit of coastal life, from exhilarating adventures to peaceful downtime. Come explore the many facets of aquatic adventures along this breathtaking stretch of the Adriatic and Ionian shores with us.

# CHAPTER FOUR

## Cultural Odyssey: Ottoman and Communist Heritage

The narrative of Albania's rich cultural heritage is entwined with the legacies of the Communist era and the Ottoman Empire. You are about to take an engrossing journey through time as you examine this beautiful tapestry. It is expected that the many historical facets that have helped Albania become the unique and resilient nation that it is today will become visible during this cultural tour.

All over Albania, the marvels of architecture, the customs of cuisine, and cultural practices have the resonance of the Ottoman Empire, which once ruled over the Balkans. Experience the unique allure of Ottoman history to the fullest by meandering through old bazaars that are adorned with vibrant colors of textiles, artisan crafts, and spices. The magnificent Ottoman-era mosques and palaces pay homage to the architectural genius of the empire, and each structure symbolizes a different period in Albania's history.

With the Ottoman era coming to an end, Albania's environment bears the distinct mark of the Communist heritage, ushering in a new chapter. Examine the remnants of the Hoxha administration, which ruled at a time when Albania seemed to be among the world's most isolated countries. Dispersed around the countryside, the bunkers that once symbolized a country always on high alert now stand as silent reminders of a bygone era. Investigate the propaganda-filled monuments and museums to learn more about the intricacies of a civilization that has managed to overcome ideological fervor.

You will have the chance to engage with the stories that are woven into Albania's very fabric by taking part in this cultural adventure. This will bring you a more nuanced understanding of a nation that has weathered historical storms. Every element, from the skyscraping minarets to the scattered concrete bunkers throughout the terrain, demonstrates the resilience and adaptability of people who have come to terms with their past while forging on into the future.

Get ready to be mesmerized by Albania's living history, where views of the mountains and cobblestone lanes resonate with the echoes of empires and ideologies. An interactive tour called "The Cultural Odyssey: Ottoman and Communist Heritage" invites you to peel back the layers of time and see the ebb and flow of Albania's captivating story.

# Historical Landmarks

Take a fascinating tour of Albania's historical sites, where each location reveals a different aspect of the country's rich and varied past. Explore Albania's history via these artifacts that attest to millennia of civilizations and cultural changes.

## Butrint: A Multicultural Tapestry

The starting point of our journey is Butrint, a UNESCO World Heritage Site that serves as a dynamic representation of the rise and fall of civilizations. The archaeological wonders of Butrint, which are tucked away on the banks of the Vivari Channel, provide windows into a history spanning from the classical Greek and Roman to the Byzantine and Ottoman periods. You will get fully immersed in the ruins of the several civilizations that once flourished in this seaside sanctuary as you walk through the Roman baths, Venetian tower, and historic theater. Butrint is more than just a site of ruins; it's a trip through time that provides an understanding of the interdependencies among the civilizations that influenced the area.

## Citadel of Stone: Gjirokastër Castle

Gjirokastër Castle, perched atop a hill, dominates the town's skyline. Gjirokastër is a historic place. With roots in the twelfth century, this stronghold has seen the rise and fall of several civilizations. You will come across reminders of Ottoman tyranny and the fight for freedom as you make your way through its stone rooms and passageways. A military museum in Gjirokastër Castle preserves items and stories that highlight the sacrifices made by Albanians in their fight for independence. From the castle's towers, you may enjoy sweeping views of the surrounding magnificent scenery as well as the castle's strategic importance.

## The Legends and Panoramas of Rozafa Castle

Tucked up in the Albanian Alps, Rozafa Castle is a reminder of both myth and history. The foundation of the castle is claimed to have been laid by Rozafa, a woman who was imprisoned behind the walls of the stronghold to secure its stability. Admire breathtaking views of the Drin River and the untamed terrain below as you explore the castle's towers and walls. This medieval stronghold gains intrigue from the tale of

Rozafa, which encourages reflection on how myth and fact are entwined.

## Berat: The Thousand Windows City

Known for its distinctive Ottoman homes dotting its hills, Berat is a UNESCO World Heritage Site that reveals a wealth of information about its past. The neighborhoods of Mangalem and Gorica exhibit a distinctive architectural fusion in which churches and mosques cohabit together. Berat, sometimes referred to as the "City of a Thousand Windows," has an ethereal feeling because of its Ottoman mansions with white façade and plenty of windows. Discovering Berat is like to entering a dynamic museum, as the ancient structures and cobblestone roads tell stories of religious variety and cross-cultural fusion.

## Petrela Castle: An Encampment in the Heart of Nature

Our trip comes to an end at Petrela Castle, a medieval stronghold set on a hill amid lush surroundings. Because of its advantageous position, the fortress was able to defend the neighboring communities and watch trade routes. With its towers and walls open for exploration, Petrela Castle is a magnificently preserved example of Albania's medieval history. Beyond its historical importance, the castle offers a tranquil haven in the outdoors with expansive views that highlight the harmonious coexistence of Albania's stunning natural surroundings and architectural legacy.

## Apollonia: Greek Legacy Echoes

Established by Greek settlers in 600 BC, Apollonia is a massive archeological site spanning 137 hectares. Apollonia, a thriving city with a triumphal arch, library, and temples, owes much of its growth to its location on the Aous River riverside. Apollonia, which the Romans took control of in the third century BC, suffered after an earthquake in 234 AD altered its harbor. Currently, the location, adorned with the façade of a local council building, promotes exploration and offers interpretations available in both French and English.

## Skanderbeg's Bastion: Krujë Castle

Tucked up in Krujë, the castle echoes with the bravery of Skanderbeg, the 15th-century

Albanian feudal ruler who stood up to the Ottoman Empire. At the Battle of Niš, the stronghold played a crucial role as the center of Skanderbeg's rebellion. Constructed inside the citadel, the Skanderbeg Museum honors Skanderbeg's 25-year revolt and preserves his legacy. The citadel, seen on the 5000 lekë banknote, is still a steadfast symbol of defiance and patriotism.

## Durrës Amphitheatre: A Roman Monument

The largest Roman amphitheater ever built in the Balkans, the Amphitheatre of Durrës was built by Emperor Trajan in the second century AD. Ten thousand to twenty thousand spectators saw gladiator bouts in the amphitheater before earthquakes destroyed it. It is a unique monument in Albania that attests to the magnificence of Roman entertainment. Its prime location in the heart of Durrës, surrounded by ancient ruins, adds to its allure, as does the nearby historic Museum.

Every step you take while exploring these historical sites reveals a tale that speaks to the Albanian people's tenacity, inventiveness, and fortitude. The story behind these monuments is just as compelling as the surrounding scenery, and it revolves around the connectivity of civilizations, the sacrifices made in the name of freedom, and the ethnic variety inherent in architectural wonders. Albania's historical sites are more than just artifacts from the past; they are doors that open to other eras and let you connect deeply with the rich tapestry of the country's enthralling history.

# Museums and Artifacts

Take a captivating tour of Albania's museums and artifacts, where the nation's cultural tapestry is shown via the carefully chosen artifacts housed within these establishments, and history is brought to life.

## The Cradle of Albanian Learning: Korça, the National Museum of Education

Acclaimed as Albania's cultural hub, Korça is home to the National Museum of Education, a tribute to the town's pivotal role in creating the country's intellectual heritage.

Enter the historic building that formerly held the first Albanian language school, which was established on March 7, 1887, under the Ottoman Empire. The museum immerses visitors in a journey through Albania's educational icons and is located in the bustling Pedonalja, a great pedestrian street that leads to the stunning Cathedral of the Resurrection of Korça.

Discover a plethora of knowledge inside the museum's sacred hallways, including books and copies of the ancient Albanian alphabet, which are a testament to the community's commitment to preserving its linguistic heritage. The exhibits are embellished with photographs of national heroes, who played a crucial role in the establishment of the pioneering school. These photographs provide a visual tale of the struggles and triumphs that characterized the early years of Albanian education. The National Museum of Education is a lighthouse, commemorating the establishment of Albania's first school and honoring the trailblazers who paved the way for the country's cultural advancement.

The National Museum of Education beckons, inviting you to partake in the rich history of Albanian education as you explore Korça's cultural milieu. Interact with the artifacts, manuscripts, and historical artifacts that demonstrate the fervent pursuit of knowledge, and experience directly the cultural vitality that establishes Korça as a pillar of Albania's literary heritage.

## Chronicles of a Nation: National Museum of History - Tirana

As a guardian of Albania's historical narrative, the National

Museum of History in Tirana takes tourists on a tour through the eras that have shaped the nation. The museum's exhibits provide a colorful picture of Albania's past, ranging from tumultuous events of the 20th century to ancient Illyrian artifacts. Admire archaeological finds, ethnological exhibits, and antiques that honor the struggles and victories of resilient people.

## A Palette of Sacred Art at the Onufri Museum in Berat

Beneath Berat's castle, the Onufri Museum stands as a testament to Albania's rich history of religious art. Dedicated to the renowned 16th-century painter Onufri, the museum showcases an exquisite assortment of icons, sacred objects, and masterpieces that exemplify the region's spiritual heritage. Immerse yourself in the centuries-old devotional vibrant hues and fine details that characterize Albanian religious art.

## Ancient Treasures Revealed at Durrës Archaeological Museum

The archaeological treasures unearthed from the area's historic monuments are shown in Durrës'

Archaeological Museum. Explore the ancient remnants of the civilizations that had thrived on the Durrës shore, revealing everything from Greek sculptures to Roman mosaics. Every artifact has a story to tell, preserving the recollections of a bygone era and connecting the present to Albania's historical beginnings.

## Krugjë: Legacy of a National Hero at Skanderbeg Museum

The Skanderbeg Museum, housed within Krujë Castle, honors the resilient soul of Gjergj Kastrioti, well known as Skanderbeg. The museum narrates the epic tales of

Skanderbeg's conflict with the Ottoman Empire, showcasing both his military prowess and his status as an enduring symbol of Albanian identity. Experience the stormy era's echoes by admiring the national hero's personal belongings, weaponry, and documents.

## Apollonia Archaeological Museum: Unearthed Elegance - Apollonia

The Apollonia Archaeological Museum, housed among the ancient ruins of Apollonia, is home to artifacts that showcase the elegance and sophistication of this

Greek town. The museum provides a glimpse into the vibrant cultural and economic hub that Apollonia once was, via everything from sculptures and inscriptions to everyday objects. By learning more about the archeological site, you may better relate the relics to the city's well-known past.

## BunkArt, Tirana: A Tributary to Contemporary History

The vibrant capital of Albania is home to BunkArt, a museum set within a massive underground bunker constructed during the Soviet era. Once built as a hideout for Enver Hoxha, the former

143

dictator of Albania, it is now a captivating repository of the country's modern past. Explore the history of the country, from the Italian occupation to communism, as BunkArt tells the narrative of resistance set against the unusual backdrop of its past.

## Voices from the Shadows of Communism, BunkArt2, Tirana

Tucked away in the heart of Tirana, BunkArt2 stands as a somber monument to those who perished during the communist regime. This scaled-down version of BunkArt invites guests to see the activities of the Ministry of Internal Affairs at that time. The names of individuals who faced the severe convictions of the government are read out in a sorrowful voice as you walk in, reflecting the unwavering spirit of those who fought for freedom.

**The Marubi National Museum of Photography in Shkodra: Using Lenses to Capture Time**

The Marubi Museum, which is located in the picturesque Pedonalja of Shkodra, tells the tale of Albanian history through the eyes of the Marubi family. The museum, which was founded by Italian painter and photographer Pietro Marubbi, shows how photography developed in Albania. Discover the vibrant fabric of Albanian life via street scenes, public events, and the first photograph taken in 1858.

Explore Albania's museums and artifacts, where each display tells a story of perseverance, ingenuity, and the nation's enduring spirit. These cultural archives act as guardians of Albania's past, inspiring tourists to discover the stories hidden inside each artifact and cultivating a deep respect for the abundant heritage of this amazing area.

## Reflections of Ottoman and Communist Influence

Albania, with its mountainous mountains and rich cultural tapestry, bears the unmistakable fingerprints of both Ottoman and Communist regimes. The interaction of these historical forces has created the nation's character, leaving behind tangible reflections that entice tourists to study the nuances of Albania's history.

# Navigating Albania's Historical Crossroads

Albania is at the crossroads of history, where the legacy of Ottoman domination and Communist ideology clash. This chapter encourages you to examine the concrete traces left by these two great forces, unraveling the threads that weave together Albania's complicated historical fabric.

## Ottoman Heritage: Palimpsest of Architectural Splendors

- Cities and Towns: Ottoman Urban Planning

Discover the Ottoman impact engraved into the urban landscapes of Albanian cities and villages. From the labyrinthine bazaars to the renowned mosques and hammams, each architectural jewel offers a narrative of Ottoman aesthetics and urban planning.

- Ottoman Fortifications: Bastions of Power

Journey through the majestic Ottoman walls that previously defended important sites. Explore the architectural brilliance that defended Albania's important locations, offering an insight into the military techniques implemented throughout this century.

- Ottoman Cuisine: Culinary Crossroads

Delve into the culinary history created by centuries of Ottoman dominance. Explore the tastes, smells, and culinary traditions that highlight the blend of Ottoman and Albanian culinary pleasures, creating a gourmet symphony.

## Communist Era: Echoes of Ideology and Struggle

- Enver Hoxha's Legacy: Socialist Realism in Architecture

Traverse the cityscapes defined by Socialist Realism, a visual reflection of Enver Hoxha's worldview. Examine the magnificent monuments, public structures, and sculptures that are intended to reflect Communist values and the cult of personality.

- Bunkers of Albania: Concrete Remnants of Isolation

Embark on a tour through the concrete bunkers spread over the Albanian terrain. These remnants, created during the Communist period, serve as mute testimony to Albania's isolationist policies and the widespread atmosphere of suspicion.

- Cultural Revolution: Impact on Arts and Education

Explore the influence of the Cultural Revolution on Albania's creative and educational realms. Uncover the developments in creative expression, literature, and education as the Communist dictatorship worked to shape minds and build ideological devotion.

As you journey through the relics of Ottoman and Communist influence, you will observe the dynamic interaction of tradition and ideology. Albania's historical mosaic is a monument to the endurance of its people, who have accepted, evolved, and emerged from the furnace of history with a unique identity. Join us as we explore the layers of Albania's history, as echoes of empires and ideologies resound across time.

# CHAPTER FIVE

## New Air Routes and Accessibility

Albania is on the cusp of a tourism revolution; it was once a hidden gem hidden deep inside the Balkans. The world is becoming more accessible because of the recent establishment of new flight routes and significant accessibility improvements. This chapter attempts to tell the intriguing story of how this increase in connectivity is causing a shift and putting Albania on the map as a popular travel destination. Come along on an adventure that invites visitors to see Albania's diverse landscapes and discover the secrets hidden inside its intricate cultural tapestry.

## Overview of Air Routes

Albania's aviation industry is now going through a revolutionary phase. Leading the way in this shift is Wizz Air, the largest and greenest airline globally. Wizz Air has announced, in a historic move, that it would be expanding its operations by introducing the cutting-edge A321neo aircraft to its Tirana base. This purchase, which becomes the airline's 11th and most contemporary aircraft in its fleet, marks a significant advancement in improving connectivity and accessibility to and from Albania.

The introduction of three new flights from Tirana to important European destinations is the result of Wizz Air's remarkable capacity increase made possible by the deployment of the A321neo. With the addition of new routes from Tirana to Bremen, Germany, Valencia, Spain, and Thessaloniki,

Greece, Wizz Air's commitment to growing its presence in the region is evident as the total number of airline flights from Albania now stands at an incredible 56.

Valeria Bragarenco, the manager of communication, emphasizes the airline's commitment to its Albanian clientele, emphasizing that this calculated move would enable them to operate 56 flights to 15 European nations and beyond. In addition to enhancing travel, the investment is intended to catalyze increased tourism in Albania, opening up new opportunities for local businesses and communities.

The choice to locate the new aircraft in Tirana is in line with Wizz Air's ongoing objective to expand its service offerings in Albania. The move highlights the importance of aviation as a catalyst for tourist and economic growth and demonstrates the airline's faith in the Albanian market. The CEO of Tirana Airport, Piervittorio Farabbi, praises Wizz Air's commitment and notes that the airline's increased capacity and routes will provide customers with more alternatives, which will help the region's tourist and business sectors grow.

Along with adding new routes, Wizz Air is increasing the frequency of its ten existing routes from Tirana as part of its expansion. Raising the frequency of flights is part of the ambitious goal to meet the growing demand from travelers. The new lines will start operating methodically on August 14th, when service from Tirana to Thessaloniki begins. Four flights every week will guarantee a perfect connection on

Mondays, Wednesdays, Fridays, and Sundays.

In addition, the routes to Bremen, Germany, and Valencia, Spain, are scheduled to launch simultaneously on December 19, 2023, providing eager tourists with more options for year-end getaways. The rise represents economic advancement in addition to providing travelers with more convenience. Hundreds of new jobs are expected to be created by Wizz Air's investment, increasing local employment opportunities and strengthening the company's commitment to the Albanian market.

With Ryanair's entry into the market and Wizz Air's efforts, Albania is now more accessible than before. New flights to the capital Tirana from Edinburgh, Manchester, and Stansted highlight the growing interest of major airlines in Albania's budding tourism sector. Together, these additional airline routes are changing the tourism scene and promoting Albania as a destination that is becoming more and more alluring to travelers due to its rich cultural diversity, stunning natural surroundings, and friendly people.

To sum up, the overview of Albania's aviation routes bears evidence of the country's increasing appeal on the global stage. The arrival of the state-of-the-art A321neo aircraft highlights Wizz Air's strategic expansion and marks a historic moment in the history of aviation in Albania. In addition to appealing to passengers' wanderlust, the extended routes and higher aircraft frequency have the potential to boost the local economy.

More people are becoming aware of Albania's alluring landscape, rich cultural heritage, and vibrant populace as it becomes more attainable. Together with Ryanair's entry, the deal between Wizz Air and Tirana Airport represents a coordinated attempt to establish Albania as an important player in the international tourism industry. The new routes are avenues for opportunity, growth, and shared experiences rather than just a system of transportation connections.

This panorama captures an era of change for Albania when the skies above the country serve as more than just flight paths; they are also conduits of connection, strengthening Albania's ties to the rest of the world. The next sections will go further into the specifics of these flight paths, revealing the unique characteristics of every location and highlighting the faultless vacation experiences they provide. Come along on this aerial journey with us as we investigate how Albania's growing accessibility is ushering in a new era of tourism and discovery.

# Increased Accessibility for Travelers

The arrival of new flight routes in Albania signifies a revolutionary era for accessibility, unleashing unprecedented options for tourists seeking to find the nation's hidden jewels. Wizz Air, a pioneering force in the aviation business, has staged a strategic expansion, bringing the state-of-the-art A321neo aircraft to its Tirana base. This step exceeds the typical sense of flight additions; it signals the commencement of a skyward revolution, boosting accessibility for a worldwide audience.

The acquisition of the A321neo, the 11th aircraft in Wizz Air's fleet, serves as a testimony to the airline's dedication to reimagining travel experiences. This strategic initiative is not only about linking airports; it's about stitching together a tapestry of choices for people eager to see the different landscapes and cultural riches of Albania. The three new routes from Tirana to Bremen, Germany, Valencia, Spain, and Thessaloniki, Greece, serve as gates to a plethora of activities, enhancing Albania's attraction.

Communication Manager Valeria Bragarenco stresses the enormous effect of this effort on Albanian travelers, providing them with a choice of 56 flights to 15 European countries and beyond. The emphasis is not only on increasing routes; it's about building relationships, both for tourists and local businesses. The notion is founded on the transforming impact of travel, generating symbiotic connections that transcend boundaries.

The decision to dedicate a new aircraft to Tirana resonates with Wizz Air's confidence in the

Albanian market. The strategic addition is a catalyst for expanded capacity and routes, offering a new wave of opportunities for passengers and promoting tourist and economic development in the area. CEO of Tirana Airport, Piervittorio Farabbi, confirms this attitude, underlining the dedication to low-cost solutions and the good influence on regional development.

As the new routes expand, the skies above Albania are becoming conduits of cultural interchange, economic progress, and shared experiences. Wizz Air's commitment to expand flight frequency on current routes further underscores the rising need for affordable travel choices. The new flights to Thessaloniki, operational from August 14th, and those to Bremen, Germany, and Valencia, Spain, from December 19, 2023, underline a strategic timeframe that matches with passengers' demands.

Ryanair's introduction into the scene, linking Tirana to important European towns, adds another dimension to the accessibility revolution. The joint efforts of Wizz Air and Ryanair are not merely increasing the map of airline connections; they are unfolding a new chapter for Albania's accessibility. The once-hidden gems are now within easy reach, tempting guests to go on a soaring trip, exploring the rich fabric of Albania's landscapes, history, and colorful culture.

## Airlines Serving Albania

Albania has become a guiding light for travelers searching out uncharted territories in the ever-expanding realm of international travel. In addition to revolutionizing accessibility, the introduction of new routes has attracted a wide range of airlines, each contributing to the overall sense of connectivity that permeates Albania's skies. Now let's explore the vibrant web of carriers that have grown to be essential for negotiating the aerial routes to and from this amazing place.

## 1. Wizz Air: Advancing the Astral Journey

The driving force behind Albania's aviation renaissance is Wizz Air, a major player in the sector renowned for its commitment to sustainability and innovation. Wizz Air has solidified its position as the leading airline in Albania with the arrival of the A321neo aircraft at its Tirana hub. This is a wise decision since it adds three additional flights to Bremen, Germany; Valencia, Spain; and Thessaloniki, Greece, in addition to increasing the airline's capacity. Wizz Air supports economic growth and cross-cultural exchange by investing in the future of travel in Albania in addition to aircraft.

## 2. Ryanair: An Important Role in the Sky Symphony of Albania

The network of connections across Albania has been strengthened by Ryanair's entry into the country. Ryanair, which connects Tirana to important European locations including Edinburgh, Manchester, and Stansted, has played a crucial role in creating new routes for travelers. Albania is more accessible because of the airline's important routes, which invite a larger audience to take in the wonders of this vibrant place.

## 3. The Expanding Web of Links

Albania's airspace is increasingly serving as a platform for an expanding aviation industry, all of which help the country become a more popular travel destination. Albanian aviation history is being redefined by the combined efforts of trailblazing carriers, with 56 flights connecting to 15 European countries and beyond. The number of flights is a testament to the growing demand for seamless travel experiences rather than just a logistical issue.

## 4. An Economic Growth Catalyst

Major airlines are not only convenient for travelers; they are also an indicator of economic growth. They serve as more than simply transporters; they also promote commerce, tourism, and cross-cultural exchange. The commitment to affordable solutions ensures that travel is a reality for many people and not simply a luxury for a select few. The strategic use of resources, as seen by the new plane in Tirana, shows confidence in the Albanian market's potential.

Albania is entering a new era of international connectivity thanks to the cooperation of these airlines, while the skies over the nation continue to change. The once-secret gem is now a humming resort that draws visitors from all over the world. Above the stunning surroundings of this magnificent country, the airlines serving Albania are not only transporting passengers; they are weaving a tale of adventure, discovery, and shared experiences.

# CHAPTER SIX

## Planning Your Trip to Albania in 2024

In 2024, a journey to Albania promises an enriching tapestry of experiences, seamlessly interwoven with breathtaking scenery, fascinating history, and a diverse culture. This book serves as your gateway to a region where ancient customs harmonize with modern allure, and where each turn reveals a new facet of this extraordinary destination. Join us on a virtual expedition to explore the essential elements of planning your remarkable trip to Albania, catering to travelers of all levels of experience.

## Best Times to Visit

Choosing the right time to visit Albania adds an extra element of enchantment to the overall trip and makes embarking on an adventure there an exciting experience. This book, which reveals the subtleties of Albania's seasons, will help you plan an impeccable vacation around the country's many landscapes and cultural riches.

June through August is when the Summer Symphony takes place.

Enjoyments of the High Season: From June to August, when Albania's allure reaches its zenith, you'll be welcomed into a world of fantastic weather and vibrant activities. You may expect temperatures in the upper 80s to upper 90s when traveling along the popular Albanian Riviera. During this time, enjoying the cuisine of Albania, going on beach excursions, and learning about the history of the nation are all suggested activities.

Aquatic Adventures: Take a break from the summer's heat in the Blue Hole, where the cool waters provide a welcome respite from the heat. Swim, play in the water, and enjoy the sun on the serene beaches while you explore the seas. Even though prices might go up at this busy time of year, overall affordability offers a fantastic experience.

November to February: Winter Wonderland

Relax and Have Fun:

November through February is a great time to be alone in the crisp winter air if you want that. For travelers on a tight budget, this is the ideal season since hotel rates have reached an all-time low. Temperatures in the coastal lowlands might be in the low 40s and near freezing in the alpine regions, depending on the location you have chosen.

Comfortable Getaways:

Look at a variety of hotels and apartments that range in price from $47 to $90 per night during these warmer months. The allure of Albania's winter combined with cost-effective options makes for a pleasant getaway that won't break the bank.

Calm Moments: April through June and September through October

Serenity of Shoulder Season:

Throughout April through June and September through October, get away from the bustling crowds and enjoy serene moments. The shoulder seasons, which fall just before and after the major summer season, provide excellent weather, less tourist traffic, and reasonably priced accommodation. Enjoy lovely temperatures between 60°F and 75°F in April through June and between 66°F and 74°F in September through October.

Sunset Bliss:

The best months to visit the Albanian Riviera for a beach vacation are June and September. The water is still a comfortable temperature, providing the ideal setting for a leisurely swim.

Gloomy days from November to December

Steering Clear of the Rain:

The worst months to go to Albania are November through December, especially in the highlands where it is rainy and chilly. Extensive research is impeded by cooler temperatures, more precipitation, and activity restrictions throughout this season. Await the arrival of the shoulder season in April, which brings a welcome burst of warmth.

## Travel Essentials and Tips

It is necessary to equip yourself with essential equipment and insider knowledge before embarking on an incredible tour in Albania. These travel tips will serve as your guide, walking you through the essentials and sensible practices for a faultless and rewarding trip.

## Advice on Packing: Must-Haves for Every Traveler

- Attire Fit for the Weather: -Summer: Sunscreen, swimwear, and breezy clothing. -Winter: Warm accessories, a waterproof jacket, and layered clothing.
- Footwear: - Sturdy, cozy shoes for strolls and excursions.

- Travel Adapters: - Make sure you use the appropriate power adapters to keep your devices charged.

- Reusable Water Bottle: - Avoid single-use plastic while staying hydrated on your travels.

- Language Guide: - A compact phrasebook in Albanian for everyday communication.

- Travel Insurance: - All-inclusive protection against unexpected events and urgent medical attention.

- Power Bank: - Make sure your gadgets are charged,

especially while going on outdoor excursions.

## Delicious Foods and Nutritional Requirements

- Local Cuisine Exploration: - Savor the distinctive cuisine of Albania, highlighting dishes like tave kosi (yogurt and lamb casserole) and byrek (pastry stuffed with cheese or meat).
- Allergens and Dietary Restrictions:

  – It is important to properly communicate dietary

preferences, since certain traditional foods may include allergens.

- Tap Water Caution: - Although tap water is often safe in large cities, in more remote areas you may want to consider bottled water.

## Traversing Regional Traditions

- Greeting Etiquette: Customary greetings include a firm handshake and direct eye contact.
- Cultural Respect: When visiting places of worship, dress modestly and get

permission before taking pictures of the occupants.

- Tipping Customs: Although not required, tipping is appreciated. Typically, the bill is rounded up.

## A Guide to Transportation

- Public Transportation: Cost-effective transportation is made possible by well-connected major city bus and minibus networks.
- Car Rentals: To ensure greater independence, think about renting a car for longer trips.

- Cab Awareness: Before getting into a cab, haggle over the fare and make sure the meter is running while traveling inside cities.

## Health and Safety Measures

- Emergency Numbers: Learn the emergency numbers and hospital names in your area.
- Travel immunizations: Before departing, ask your healthcare provider about the required vaccines.
- Money Exchange: When obtaining local currency, especially in tourist areas,

use reliable exchange services.

- Local SIM Card: Use a local SIM card to maintain communication and data connectivity.

**Exciting Adventures and Outdoor Discoveries**

- Hiking Essentials: For Albania's scenic paths, sturdy hiking boots, a map, and enough of water are essential.

- Beach Preparedness: For beach holidays, include essentials like swimwear, a beach towel, and sunscreen.

- Cultural Events Calendar: To enhance your cultural experiences, look for festivals and events on your community's calendars.

Equipped with these fundamental travel tips and insider knowledge, you'll be well-prepared for an interesting and rewarding journey across Albania's diverse landscapes and rich cultural legacy. I wish you a journey filled with incredible experiences and new learnings.

# Recommendations for an Unforgettable Experience

Take into consideration these suggestions that will give your trip to Albania more depth and richness to ensure that it is nothing short of extraordinary.

## Accept Warm Local Welcome:

Albanians are known for being amiable and welcoming. Seize the opportunity to socialize, tell stories, and experience customary hospitality. A genuine glimpse into Albanian life may be had in homestays and locally owned hotels.

## Look for Hidden Treasures:

Even while popular locations have their charm, go off the main path to uncover undiscovered gems. For those willing to go beyond the popular tourist destinations, peaceful mountain towns, hidden beaches, and unspoiled scenery await.

## Indulge in Sophisticated Flavors:

Albanian food is a symphony of flavors drawn from Balkan and Mediterranean customs. Venture beyond the typical and discover local delights. Explore regional markets, enroll in cooking classes, and sample the diverse cuisine that distinguishes each region of the country.

## Occasions and Customary Events:

Plan your trip to coincide with regional celebrations and cultural gatherings to see Albania's vibrant traditions. From energetic music festivals to historic celebrations, these occasions provide a unique window into Albanian culture.

## Examining History and Culture:

Explore the rich history of Albania by going to medieval castles, Ottoman heritage sites, and ancient ruins. To add context and richness to your cultural experience, interact with local guides to learn about the stories that surround each monument.

## Outdoor Adventures and Scenic Drives:

Albania's diverse landscapes are worth exploring. Take nice drives across mountainous terrain, go climbing, or enjoy water sports along the picturesque coastline. The greatest way to enjoy

Albania's natural beauty is to go on outdoor adventures.

**Establish a Nature Connection:**

Albania is a haven for lovers of the natural world. Lakes, mountain ranges, and national parks provide opportunities for hiking, bird viewing, and just taking in the breathtaking surroundings. Spend some time appreciating Albania's unique natural wonders.

**Customs and Cultural Etiquette:**

To build long-lasting relationships with the Albanian people, observe customs and manners in the area. Acquire some basic vocabulary in Albanian, understand customary salutations, and recognize the cultural nuances that add depth to your interactions.

## Take Pictures, Tell Tales:

Carry a camera or smartphone with you, and capture the moments that speak to you. These images will become treasured keepsakes of your trip to Albania, whether it's the vibrant colors of the local markets, the expansive vistas of the countryside, or the beautiful details of historical landmarks.

## Have an open mind and remain curious:

Be curious and have an open mind when you go to Albania. Accept the unexpected, take part in spur-of-the-moment conversations, and allow Albania's rhythm to guide your journey. Most of the time, the most priceless memories are often the spontaneous ones.

With its unique blend of nature, history, and culture, Albania invites you to have a wonderful holiday. You're guaranteed to create a tale that lingers long after your journey is over if you fully immerse yourself in the local culture and take advantage of this Balkan gem. Happy travels!

# CHAPTER SEVEN

## Albania in 2024: A Rising Star

Albania is a rising star among the world's tourist destinations, drawing travelers with its unique charm and captivating landscapes. The nation is now going through a revolutionary journey, opening new air routes, improving accessibility, and appreciating its rich cultural heritage.

Wizz Air's expanded flight options and Ryanair's newly launched routes have increased Albania's accessibility to unprecedented levels, facilitating travelers' exploration of the country's many regions. Travelers looking for an immersive and captivating experience will find a fascinating setting among the nation's ancient buildings, vibrant festivals, and breathtaking natural wonders.

This chapter discusses Albania's evolving history, highlighting the country's modern achievements, rich cultural heritage, and range of opportunities for travelers desiring to take in the breathtaking Balkan scenery. Accompany us as we explore Albania's allure in 2024—a country poised to emerge as a major player in the global tourist scene.

# Recent Developments and Recognition

Albania has adopted many crucial structural reforms that have the potential to completely transform its economic system, putting the country on the verge of a revolution. The cornerstone of the country's post-challenges recovery strategy is represented by these adjustments, which are intended to promote equitable development, increase productivity, and improve competitiveness. Following the 2019 earthquake, the global COVID-19 pandemic, and economic instability, Albania is concentrating its efforts on reviving key sectors, with tourism, agriculture, and digitization taking precedence.

Albania's approach is characterized by a strong emphasis on ecologically beneficial measures. This demonstrates a dedication to sustainable practices in line with the pressing need to combat climate change on a worldwide scale. An impressive 4.8% growth rate was recorded in 2022, demonstrating the resilience of the Albanian economy. Growing private consumption, strong exports, and astute investments enabled this boom to overcome obstacles caused by rising food and energy prices.

The narrative surrounding Albania's economic recovery is closely associated with the country's resolve to eradicate poverty. The nation forecasts a continuous decline in poverty rates as employment opportunities grow and earnings rise. But even with the tourism sector's notable growth, 2023 is expected to be a year of economic contraction.

Albania's efforts have not been disregarded internationally in addition to the local arena. Recognition on a global scale, including collaborative efforts with esteemed institutions such as the World Bank and other associates, indicates a shared dedication to bolstering Albania's ultimate objective. These alliances work to overcome obstacles, implement structural adjustments, and encourage fiscal consolidation in order to promote long-term economic development.

## Anticipated Highlights for 2024

The Extended Assembly of the Socialist Party of Albania took place in Pogradec, Albania, on a frigid November day at a pivotal juncture that prepared Prime Minister Edi Rama to unveil an ambitious fiscal plan that would last until 2024. The main focus of Rama's speech was a substantial financial commitment of 400 million euros intended to increase public sector wages, to raise the average pay to a whopping 900 euros.

In addition to showcasing Albania's commitment to economic resilience, the assembly highlighted the country's standing as one of the region's most robust economies, as confirmed by an evaluation by the International Monetary Fund (IMF). Rama emphasized the country's ability to deal with unforeseen issues like pandemics and earthquakes while continuing on a steady path of prosperity and bringing down its debt to around 60%. A key component of Rama's agenda is an appeal for local investment, urging Albanians to reinvest their money domestically. One real-world success story that was shared was how a tower in Bulqizë was transformed into a popular tourist destination, demonstrating the advantages of local investment.

The 2024 budget proposal has not, however, been exempt from criticism. The leader of the Alliance for the Future of Kosovo, Ramush Haradinaj, expressed concerns about the region's underdevelopment and stagnation and issued a dire warning about ultimate impoverishment. This range of viewpoints highlights the political controversy around the budget and its alleged impact on economic growth.

The transparency with which the Horseracing Integrity and Safety Authority provision was handled throughout the budget talks is an intriguing aspect of the proceedings. The Federal Trade Commission's proactive efforts to gather public feedback demonstrate its dedication to inclusive decision-making, which promotes democratic governance. As we go through the next chapters, we uncover the anticipated highlights for 2024 and explore the revolutionary potential concealed in Albania's economic strategies as well as the shifting landscape of political reactions and public participation.

# CONCLUSION

As we draw to a close our exploration of Albania, it is important to reiterate why you should plan your next vacation there. Albania, tucked away in the center of the Balkans, offers a wealth of diverse landscapes, a wealth of historical significance, and a welcoming demeanor. Albania offers a variety of experiences for every type of visitor, from the rugged grandeur of its mountainous landscape to the sun-kissed beaches of the Adriatic and Ionian shores.

The historical echoes of Ottoman and Communist legacies, the enduring allure of beach towns, and the cultural treasures housed in its museums and antiquities have all been explored in the pages of this book. We have traveled through the expanding accessibility via new flight paths, seen the economic resilience shown by previous innovations, and predicted the anticipated highlights for 2024.

We've discovered the best times to visit, essential travel tips, and suggestions for an incredible experience during our journey across this beautiful country. Now a bright spot on the travel map, Albania used to be a hidden gem that beckoned travelers to explore its wonders.

In closing, I would like to extend an invitation to you, my reader, to embark on your Albanian adventure. Albania extends a warm welcome to all travelers, regardless of experience level. You are free to discover its people's warmth, the richness of its culture, and the breathtaking vistas that lie ahead.

We bid adieu to Albania's breathtaking scenery and rich cultural legacy and invite you to turn the key to begin your new adventure. This may be the end of the adventure, but Albania's magic continues to beckon, waiting for you to write your own story within its ancient embrace. I hope your exploration of Albania proves to be as enthralling and amazing as the nation itself. Safe travels.

Printed in Great Britain
by Amazon